PREACHING
JOB

Talk outlines for the book of Job

CONTENTS

A. QUICK HELP: How to prepare a talk on Job *4*

B. How to use *Preaching Job* 5

C. About the book of Job 7

D. Study and preach Job 9

E. Lessons from Job 46

F. Reasons for suffering 47

Preaching Job is published by The Good Book Company
© Phil Crowter/The Good Book Company 2010

email: ppp@thegoodbook.co.uk

Websites
UK: www.thegoodbook.co.uk
N America: www.thegoodbook.com
Australia: www.thegoodbook.com.au
New Zealand: www.thegoodbook.co.nz

Unless indicated, all Scripture references are taken from the HOLY BIBLE, NEW INTERNATIONAL VERSION. Copyright © 1973, 1978, 1984 International Bible Society. Used by permission.

ISBN: 9781907377297 • Printed in Poland.

The *Pray Prepare Preach* project is working in partnership with a growing number of organisations worldwide, including: Langham Partnership • Grace Baptist Mission • Pastor Training International (PTI) • Sovereign World Trust • Africa Inland Mission (AIM) • Worldshare • Entrust Foundation • India Bible Literature • African Pastors' Book Fund • Preacher's Help • African Christian Textbooks (ACTS) Nigeria • Orphans for Christ, Uganda • Project Timothy.

Also in this series:
Preaching God's Big Story • Preaching Mark • Preaching Philippians

Please read this first!

It is a big joy to bring you another PPP book. We pray that this will help you to preach God's word. We want people everywhere to hear God's word clearly. Then people will turn to Jesus. Christians will grow more like Jesus. God will have all the praise.

We give you a lot of help. But you must still work hard! Please do not just copy what you read!

PPP means Pray! Prepare! Preach! There is a lot to do before you preach.

PRAY. The best talk in the world is no good without God. Pray that you will speak God's truth. Pray that God will speak to people's hearts. Pray for yourself as you prepare. Pray that God's word will come alive to you.

PREPARE. You need several hours to prepare a Bible talk. Work hard to understand the Bible section. Think about the help that we have given you. Which parts will help your listeners? How can you explain it better? We only give you a few words. You need to say more, so that everyone understands.

PREACH. Now you can preach. It is a big joy when we know that we teach God's words. These are not things that we want to say. These are God's truths, written in his word. God has promised that they will do his work!
Isaiah 55:10-11

Here is the best way to use this book. Start at the beginning of Job and teach each section in turn.

Phil Crowter

Phil Crowter wrote this book in his last few months of suffering with cancer. Like Job, he knew about suffering. Soon after finishing this, he died and went to be with Jesus. Some of these messages were the last he preached. If you have access to the Internet, his sermons are available at www.cuckfieldbaptistchurch.co.uk/Pages/Job2.html

A. QUICK HELP:
How to prepare a talk on Job

1. Pray for God's help.

▼

2. 📖 **Read the Bible section several times.**
Use ⊡ **Background** to help you to understand the section. Use
⊡ **Notes** to help you to understand difficult Bible verses.

▼

3. Try to find the main point that God is teaching us in the Bible section.
Use ⊡ **Main point** to help you.

▼

4. Pray for your people. Think how this Bible section will help them.
Use ⊛ **Something to work on** to help you.

▼

5. Write your talk in your own language. Start with the main points which the Bible teaches.
Use our notes in the **PREACH** section to help you.

▼

6. Now write a beginning and an end for your talk.

▼

7. Check what you have done.
- Is the **main point** clear?
- Do you show them what the **Bible** teaches?
- Do you use **word pictures** to help your people understand and remember?
- Do you **connect** with the people?
- What do you hope will **change?**

▼

8. Pray that God will speak through your words. Pray that his truth will change people.

For more help read the next section.

B: How to use *Preaching Job*

Every time you prepare a talk, begin with these things:

- Pray for God's help.

- Read the Bible section.

- Try to find the main point that God is teaching us in the Bible section.

Then you can use these notes to help you. There are two pages for each talk. The first page helps you to think about the Bible section. The second page gives you headings and ideas for a talk.

When you see this symbol  , you need to read what the Bible says.

STUDY PAGE: Understand the Bible

The first page helps you to understand the Bible section.

◉ Background

It is important to think about what comes before and after the section. We will not look at every chapter of Job. But we need to understand how each part fits into the book.

The **Background** section will help you to do this.

Ask how a section is like other things that you have read in Job. Ask how it helps our understanding of suffering.

◉ Main point

We have put the most important point in a few words. Think about this point. Can you see that this is what the Bible section is teaching? Try to make sure that this point is very clear in your talk.

✦ Something to work on

This section chooses something from the Bible section, which you need to think about. It is important to work hard to understand the Bible. Think carefully about how to teach the point in this section.

◉ Notes

This section tells you about difficult Bible verses. It will help you not to make mistakes when you are teaching.

PREACH PAGE:
Teach the Bible

The second page helps you to teach the Bible section. You must also do your own work. This page gives you ideas. You must take the ideas and use them in the best way. We give you the bones, but you must put the meat on the bones!

1. THINGS WE HAVE WRITTEN TO HELP YOU

• **Two or three headings.**

These are written **LIKE THIS.** These headings will help you to teach the Bible clearly. You can change the headings to make them better for your people.

• **We show you what the Bible says.** We want people to listen to the Bible. Keep reminding them of what the Bible says. If they have a Bible, ask them to find the verse you are talking about. This symbol 📖 will help you know when to do this.

• **We explain what the Bible is teaching.** You need to think how to explain the Bible so that your people understand. You know your people. We do not know your people. Your words are better than our words.

• **We sometimes use a word picture.** Here is an example from the notes on Job 1:1-5:

⊕ *Jesus says to his people, "You are the light of the world". They shine like the sun. Real Christians shine because they have light inside. Their goodness shines out when people behave badly round them. They do not copy the people round them.*

Sometimes, the word picture may not be good for your people. A Bible teacher must find a better word picture to help the people understand. You will need to find many more word pictures to help teach the Bible truth. Be very careful that the word picture teaches what the Bible is saying.

• **We show you how to connect the Bible teaching to your people.** It is important to hear God's word speaking **to us.** We need to know how the Bible teaching changes us.

• **We give you one or two ideas.** You need to think of more ways to connect the Bible to your people. You know the people. You know how the Bible needs to change their lives. Here is an example:

> 🔊 *Has God made you good on the inside? Or do you just look like a Christian when you are at church? If you want to be a **real** Christian, Jesus is the only person who can change you.*

2. OTHER THINGS YOU WILL NEED TO DO

- **Think how to start your talk.** Your people need to see why it is important to listen today. Tell them what you will teach them from the Bible. Tell them why it is important for them.

- **Think how to end your talk.** Remind them of the main points. Give them something to think about or something to do.

- **Pray!** You are telling the people God's truth from God's word. Pray that God will use your words to speak to the people. Pray that God's truth will change people.

- **Always use your own language. Never** say things in English if the people do not speak English well.

C. About the book of Job

Job is a very important book for Christians because it is about suffering. Suffering comes to all of us in different ways, so this book is for us all.

Job is not an easy book to read, so many Christians do not know it very well. *Preaching Job* will help you to bring this book to your listeners. It will teach them important truths about suffering. This will help them when suffering comes to them.

We do not know when Job lived but many people think this is one of the earliest books of the Bible. Job is one of the "wisdom" or "poetry" books of the Bible.

The first two chapters and the last chapter tell the story of Job's suffering. The rest of the book is talking.

SUMMARY

At first, Job praises God, as God takes away his possessions, children and health. But as time goes on, Job struggles with his suffering. His friends accuse him of doing wrong and Job knows that this is not true. But Job does not understand why then he suffers. It does not seem fair to Job. Worst of all, God is silent. God does not comfort Job. God does not say that Job is innocent.

Job says many strong things in his suffering (and wrong things too).

Mostly he feels dark and depressed. He feels that God is against him. But he never lets go of God (as Satan wants him to). Flashes of deep trust in God shine through Job's painful words.

Job's friends do not help him. Their long arguments are hard to follow but the main point is to show that Job must have sinned. Job's friends tell him to repent and turn back to God. This does not help because sin is not Job's problem.

In the end, God speaks. This humbles Job and shows him that he does not need the answers to his questions. Instead he learns to trust that his great God is good and just.

LESSONS

There are many important lessons to learn from this book. (See the discussion page at the back—"Lessons from Job", page 48. Look at these lessons now and keep them in mind as you teach Job.)

An outline of the book of Job

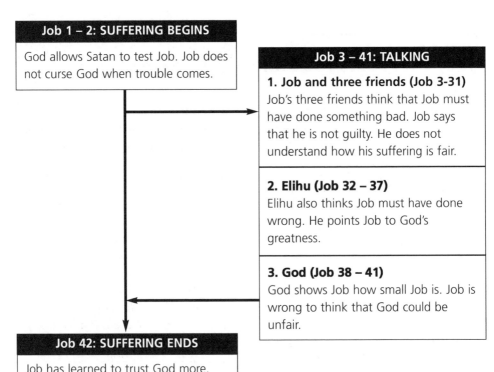

Job 1 – 2: SUFFERING BEGINS
God allows Satan to test Job. Job does not curse God when trouble comes.

Job 3 – 41: TALKING

1. Job and three friends (Job 3-31)
Job's three friends think that Job must have done something bad. Job says that he is not guilty. He does not understand how his suffering is fair.

2. Elihu (Job 32 – 37)
Elihu also thinks Job must have done wrong. He points Job to God's greatness.

3. God (Job 38 – 41)
God shows Job how small Job is. Job is wrong to think that God could be unfair.

Job 42: SUFFERING ENDS
Job has learned to trust God more. God blesses him with more than before.

PREACHING
JOB

D: Study and preach the book of Job

1 A GOOD MAN

▣ Background

We may have questions about suffering. Satan also has a question to ask. "Does Job only serve God because it gets him many things?" 📖 *Job 1:9-11*

God answers that question right at the beginning. Job is good not just because that makes him rich! Job really is good. He is good inside 📖 *Job 1:1-5.*

(When God says that Job is good [Job 1:1, 8], he does not mean that Job never sins! Job has a heart that knows and loves God. Job is good **inside**.)

⊡ Main point

Job, who will suffer terrible things, is good from his heart.

⊠ Something to work on

What Satan says (Job 1:9-11) is not true for Job. But it is true for many people. Many people want to be Christians because they think they will have better lives. They think that God will bless them. They want the good things that God gives.

Help your listeners to see that this is not right. People who think like this are not like Job. They are not true Christians.

▣ Notes

• **Job 1:1.** Job was not perfect, but he was "blameless" (people saw nothing wrong in him) and "upright" (good). He "feared" (loved and worshipped) God. He "shunned" (turned away from) evil.

• **Job 1:2-3.** Job was the "greatest" (richest) man in that part of the world. People saw Job's wealth and knew that God had blessed him. In the **Old Testament**, God promised to give good things to his people when they followed him; (see Deuteronomy 28:1-14*).* Today, if someone is rich, it does **not** mean that God has blessed them. God's blessing shows when someone is "rich in faith" (James 2:5). We are "rich" when we know God and belong to his kingdom.

• **Job 1:4-5.** This shows how careful Job was about sin. He did not know if his children had done anything wrong. But he knew that sin needed a sacrifice. (Job fears that his children may turn away from ["curse"] God in their fun.)

A GOOD MAN

📖 *Job 1:1*

⊕ Jesus says to his people, "You are the light of the world". They shine like the sun. Real Christians shine because they have light inside. Their goodness shines out when people behave badly round them. They do not copy others.

Some people copy the people round them. At work, they are like the people at work. At church, they are like the people at church. But true Christians are not like this. They are lights that shine out goodness. They **are good inside.** God has changed them and made them good—as he made Job good.

Job knows God. He hates evil. He loves good. And nothing that happens to Job will change that.

> ⮞ *What if God took away your money, your house, your health, your family. Would you be like Job? Would you still trust God, love good and hate evil? Or do you only follow God when life is easy?*

God says that Job is good and true. So we know what will happen in this book! Job will stay good! God will test Job's faith, but his faith will not break.

> ⮞ *Praise God that when we become true Christians, Jesus changes us. He makes us good inside! If Jesus has made us true Christians, we will keep with God to the end. (This does not mean that we **always** do good things!)*

A GOOD, RICH MAN

📖 *Job 1:2-3*

• If you were rich, what would you do with your money? What kind of life would you live? Might you forget God?

Very few people are both good and rich. Few people love God **and** have lots of money. Job was rich **and** loved God. Look how much he owned!

God wanted everyone to see that he had blessed Job. But Job's possessions did not spoil him. He still trusted God, loved good and hated evil.

Job was a good man. When God gave him many things, Job was still a good man. When God takes everything away, Job will still be a good man. When a person is good on the inside, then outside things will not make him bad.

> ⮞ *Has God made you good on the inside? Or do you just look like a Christian when you are at church? If you want to be a **real** Christian, Jesus is the only person who can change you.* 📖 **John 3:3, 16.**

2 GOD AND SATAN

⊡ Background

God told us that Job is a good man (Job 1:1). And God tells Satan that Job is a good man (Job 1:8). God's plan is for Satan to attack Job! God wants to show Satan, and us, how a good man suffers.

📖 *Job 1:1-12*

⊡ Main point

God is in control of Satan. God is in control of the hard things that happen to us.

⊠ Something to work on

Some Christians think that good things come from God and bad things come from Satan. What is wrong with that thinking?

God brought Job trouble (Job 2:10, 42:11). When something bad happens to you, it is **hard** to believe that God has allowed it. But he has. How can you help your listeners to see that God **is** in control?

There is great comfort when we know that God is behind all our trouble. We are in God's loving hands, not the devil's hating hands.

Encourage your listeners to hold on to two important truths: God has all power **and** God is love (Psalm 62:11-12).

⊡ Notes

• **Job 1:6-7.** We do not know why Satan comes here with the angels. God threw Satan out of heaven, but God allows him to be here. God wants to use Satan's evil for God's good purposes.

• **Job 1:8. God** points Job out to Satan. **God** plans for Satan to trouble Job.

• **Job 1:9-11.** Satan speaks against **God**, as well as against Job. Satan says, "You give Job many good things. You protect ("put a hedge around") Job from all harm. That is how you keep him on your side! So of course Job serves you!"

• **Job 1:12.** God tells Satan exactly what he can do and what he cannot do. God is in control of Satan.

SATAN

SATAN IS ONLY AN EVIL ANGEL
📖 *Job 1:6*

Satan is not God. Satan cannot do what he wants to. He cannot touch Job until God allows him to.

⊕ Imagine two boys, a big one and a small one. The big boy hates the small boy and wants to hurt him. But the teacher is there. So the big boy cannot touch the other boy. The big boy is a picture of Satan. Satan is stronger than God's people and wants to hurt them. But he cannot touch us unless God says so. 📖 *Job 1:12*

> ▷ *Praise God that Satan cannot do what he wants to. Satan is not in charge of evil. He can only do what God allows him to. When bad things happen to God's people, our kind **God** is in control. Praise God!*

SATAN SEEKS EVIL
📖 *Job 1:9-11*

Do you see what Satan wants to do? He wants to spoil Job's friendship with God! He says that Job only serves God because he gets good things from God. This is a lie.

> ▷ *Satan loves to put doubts into our minds like this. Remember that the devil is a cheat, and wants to hurt us.* 📖 *James 4:7*

GOD
📖 *Job 1:6-12*

See how **God** asks Satan the questions. **God** makes Satan think about Job. **God** says that Satan can hurt Job. God is in control of everything!

After Job 2, we do not read about Satan. Satan is not very important in the book of Job. When we suffer, the important person to think about is God. **We do not blame Satan—we trust God.**

Job knows that **God** is behind everything that he suffers. Later on, Job says that even if God kills him, he will still trust God (Job 13:15).

It is hard to understand that God will let Satan do terrible things to us; 📖 *Job 1:12.* Talk about how we feel when hard things happen. See SOMETHING TO WORK ON.

> ▷ *Satan's words in Job 1:9-11 may be true for you. Will you only trust God when he gives you good things?*
> *Or do you **know** that he loves you because he gave his Son to die on the cross for you? Will you trust him, whatever happens, because Jesus died?* 📖 *Romans 5:8*

3 PRAISE GOD?

◉ Background

We know that terrible things will soon happen to Job. We know that God has allowed **Satan** to test Job—Satan wants Job to curse God when the trouble comes. We know that **God** is sure about Job—he is a true believer, a truly good man.
📖 *Job 1:1-12*

Remember, Job knows nothing about this. Here we learn how deep Job's faith is; 📖 *Job 1:13-22.*

◉ Main point

Whatever happens to a believer, it is possible to praise and trust God.

✳ Something to work on

1. Job is a wonderful example to us. But we do not always praise God in trouble as he did. Remember to comfort believers who have failed. Perhaps some have hit out against God in their pain. Help them to ask God to forgive them and learn to praise him again.

2. Before trouble comes, it is good to learn about God's ways. He is good, loving, wise and in control. When we know this, it is easier to praise him when trouble comes (Daniel 2:20-21, 4:34-35).

◉ Notes

• **Job 1:14-19.** Four terrible things happen to Job's family. Two of them are groups of men who attack ("Sabeans" and "Chaldeans"). The other two are a lightning storm and wind. We know that all four have come from Satan, with God's agreement. God is in control, so Job is right to see that God has done this (Job 1:21).

• **Job 1:20.** Job tore his clothes and cut off his hair to show his pain and loss. It is good to show our pain. Even though Job's heart is full of pain, **he still wants to praise God**. We can be real with God and show him how we feel (sad, in pain, angry). We should never **pretend** to praise God with a smile if we do not feel like that inside.

• **Job 1:22.** See Job 1:11. **Satan has failed.**

HOW WE THINK ABOUT GOD
📖 *Job 1:20*

[Tell the story. Act it out as four people run to bring the bad news to Job.] Think how you would feel if only one of these things happened to you.

You find out how you really think about God when everything goes wrong.

Think of Job before this happened. He was happy. He was rich. He loved God. Then, in a few minutes, he loses everything. He even loses all his ten children. Here we can see how Job thinks about God—

• **Job shows his pain.** He is real with God. He does not pretend that he is OK. He is not OK. He is broken to pieces inside.

• **Job worships.** Job has so much pain. He has many questions. But they must wait. **First** comes something more important than everything else. He praises God!

» *When trouble comes, do you turn* **to** *God? Or do you turn* **away** *from God? That shows what you think about God. Job turned to praise God because he knew that* **God still deserved praise**. *Whatever God does, he is* **good**, *he is* **love**. *Do you believe that?*

HOW WE THINK ABOUT GOD'S GIFTS
📖 *Job 1:21*

You find out how you really think about God's gifts when he takes them away.

Satan was so wrong (Job 1:9-11). Satan thought that Job was in love with **God's gifts**. But Job was in love with God. And when God took everything away, Job was still in love with God! 📖 *Job 1:21*

• Think of all that you have. We say, "That's mine". But is it really?

• What right do we have to our things? Who gave them to us?

» *If God takes away your health, your crops or your father, will you praise God like Job? You still have God. Will you love him?*

Even when God takes away small things, it is easy to complain or get angry. Or perhaps you get worried about your things? Do you find it hard to share or to give? So are you too much in love with God's **gifts**?

» *There is a gift that God will never take away. It is far more valuable than everything else you can own. If you do not have this gift of Jesus, ask him for it now.*
📖 *Matthew 6:19-21*

4 GOD HAS THE RIGHT

◉ Background

Terrible loss shows how real Job's faith is (Job 1:20-22):

- He praises God in his pain.

- He loves God when God takes all his gifts away.

But Satan does not give up easily. He still wants to make Job turn away from God. He wants to show that Job only serves God because of all that God gives him.

📖 *Job 2:1-10*

◉ Main point

God has the right to do anything to us. (Christians sometimes call this God's "sovereignty". He is King [sovereign] over us.)

✳ Something to work on

This truth is very hard to accept when trouble comes. Show that you understand how difficult it can be. Speak in a kind way. Remember how much some of your listeners have suffered.

Tell stories of people today who accepted trouble like Job. This will give your listeners courage and strength. It will show that this difficult truth is good truth! It helps us to hold on to God.

◉ Notes

- **Job 2:3.** God takes responsibility for what has happened to Job ("you incited me against him"). Satan asked God to let him attack Job. God could have said no. But God said yes.

- **Job 2:4-5.** (See Job 1:12.) Satan says, "This trouble has only gone skin deep. We have not really hurt Job yet. Let me hurt Job himself. Then he will curse you."

- **Job 2:9.** Job's wife sees that Job will not stop being faithful. If Job curses God, he goes against everything that he believes. Job's wife thinks that is better than this terrible pain. But she, like Job, knows that it would be wrong.

HOLD ON!

📖 *Job 2:9*

[You could show again how God sets the limits of what Satan can do (Job 2:1-6). God is in control. Satan cannot take Job's life.]

Think how much trouble Job already has! He has lost his children and his wealth. And he knows that **God** did this to him. His pain is too much.

Then God gives him more pain! Sores all over his body. Think how painful this was (Job 2:7-8)! We know that this was Satan's idea. Job does not know this, but he does know that God is always in control.

What will Job do? 📖 *Job 2:9*

Job holds on to God. His wife wants to stop trusting God. She is angry with God. She wants Job to finish with God. If God does all this to Job, then curse God! But Job holds on to God, because he knows this truth: **God has the right to do ANYTHING to us.**

Job has believed this for many years. Now, in terrible pain, he still believes it. He will not let go of God.

> ⏩ *It is easy to think like Job's wife. We think, "How can God be good if he does **this**?" We think, "If God lets all this happen, it would be better to go away from God." **But this is wrong.** It is also very dangerous.*
>
> *Job is right. When you cannot understand, hold on to God. Believe what the Bible says. God has the right to do anything to us. And he is always good.*

ACCEPT TROUBLE!

📖 *Job 2:10*

What does Job believe?

• That we should accept trouble only when we **deserve** it?

• That we should accept a **normal** amount of trouble?

• That we should accept **any** trouble, **any** time, even when we **cannot see why**?

What do you believe?

Job does not find this easy! We will see that later. But he knows that this trouble is a **gift** from God. Job does not understand it, but he **accepts** the gift from his good God.

> ⏩ *Will you trust God when he does not tell you why? God has the right to give us **any** trouble because he is God! Will you trust him? Remember that God gave his Son to suffer. Jesus suffered to **save** his people from the worst trouble—hell!*

5 FEEL HIS PAIN!

▣ Background

We begin a long section of the book of Job. For many chapters, Job and his friends argue about Job's suffering. We have to wait until the last chapter to find out what happens to Job in the end.

Satan fails to make Job sin. Job refuses to turn against God. Instead he praises God (Job 1:20-22, 2:10).

Here we see how deep Job's pain is. Job still holds on to God, but his words show his bitter pain; 📖 *Job 2:11 – 3:26.*

▣ Main point

Feel Job's pain and understand.

(This helps us to understand people today who suffer great trouble. It also helps us when we feel like Job.)

✳ Something to work on

It is easy to see what is wrong with what Job says. Of course we should not curse the day we were born! Of course we should not wish that we were dead! But don't miss the point. **Job needs to show his pain.** We need to listen to his **feelings.** When life hurts us, we need people to try to understand our suffering. We do not usually need someone to correct us.

In your talk, help your listeners to feel for people in their pain.

▣ Notes

• **Job 2:11-13.** Job's three friends really want to help Job. They cry with him. They sit in silence with him for a week.

• **Job 3:1-10.** Job curses the day he was born. He wishes that day had never happened. He wants the day taken out of the calendar.

• **Job 3:11-19.** Job says, "If only I had died at birth! Then I would not have all this pain. I would rest in peace." Life is so terrible that death seems lovely to Job! (Job is not right in Job 3:17; he forgets that death means judgement.)

• **Job 3:20-26.** Job longs for death. He would be so happy to die— why does God keep him alive? There is no escape (Job 3:23). God feeds him pain and tears! (Job 3:24) There is no rest.

FEEL HIS SILENT PAIN
📖 *Job 2:11-13*

Job is silent. Think of all that has happened to him. Job is too full of shock and terror to speak. All he can do is to sit in pain.

His friends are silent. They sit with him for a week! That shows that they really care. They do not try to talk; they share in his pain and tears.

> ⏩ *Sometimes that is all people want. Someone who takes time to be with them. Someone to cry with, to hug. That can be the best way to show God's love.*

FEEL HIS SPOKEN PAIN

It can be difficult when people speak out. All their pain pours out. They may say things that we know are not right. Perhaps they hit out at God. We need to **feel their pain**, not to correct them.

FEEL HIS DARKNESS
📖 *Job 3:3-5*

⊕ When the lights suddenly go out, everything is dark. Everything is still there, but you cannot see anything. It is like that for Job. Everything is dark. There is no comfort, no joy, no hope. Just pain. He knows that God must still be there, but he can only feel darkness.

Job still has his faith in God. He curses his birth day, but he will never curse his God! If only that day had never happened. If only he was never born! Job wants us to feel just how bad it is for him.

> ⏩ *If you feel dark like Job, then remember Jesus. Jesus knows what darkness feels like. He suffered three hours on the cross when God left him. He felt the darkness of hell. Do you know Jesus? Praise him that he took hell's darkness instead of you!*

FEEL HOW HE LONGS FOR DEATH
📖 *Job 3:20-24, 26*

Job feels so dark inside but the sun still shines on him (Job 3:20)! Why will God not let him die? Job feels as if God has put a hedge round him to make sure that he does not die. Life is like a prison. God feeds him pain and tears. He will not let Job rest!

God wants us to understand what this darkness feels like. That is why it is here in the Bible. God wants us to understand some of Job's pain.

> ⏩ *If you ever feel like Job, you do not need to give up hope. Job came through this dark time. God lets you say things like Job, even if they are not good things to say. Remember that whatever Job feels, he still holds on to God. So you hold on too!*

6 HOW NOT TO HELP!

◉ Background

In Job 4 – 5, Eliphaz speaks. Then Job replies (Job 6 – 7). Bildad speaks next, then Job again (Job 8 – 10). Job's third friend, Zophar speaks, and Job answers (11 – 14). Then Eliphaz tries again, and the pattern repeats until Job 31.

Eliphaz, Bildad and Zophar say the same kind of things. They think that Job has done something very bad—this is why he suffers so much! They all try to get him to ask God to forgive him and come back to God. But we know that they are wrong! Job 1 – 2 tells readers that Job is **good**, not bad. 📖 *Job 4–5*

◉ Main point

When you talk to someone in trouble, listen first! Do not give your own ideas, which the Bible shows are wrong!

✳ Something to work on

These three friends say many true things in the book of Job. They know a lot about God. But they also speak wrong things about God and about Job (📖 See Job 42:7). Sometimes they do say true things, but they do not fit Job. (Example: 📖 See Job 5:17-18)

Therefore we have to be careful. **All** the book of Job is the word of God. But many things that people say **in it** are wrong! We must read big sections to understand it well.

◉ Notes

The main things Eliphaz says to Job are:

- **Job 4:1-6.** You have pointed other people to God, but now I need to correct you.

- **Job 4:7-11.** I have found that people harvest the trouble that they sow.

- **Job 4:12-21.** God showed this to me: **no one is pure in God's sight.**

- **Job 5:1-7.** I have seen fools do well, and then they have great trouble. Trouble does not come from nowhere. It comes from us.

- **Job 5:8-16.** My advice is this: go to our great God with your problems!

- **Job 5:17-27.** Let God correct you, and enjoy his kind blessing again.

HOW NOT TO HELP

Job's friends really want to help Job. But they are too proud of what **they** think, and what **they** want to say. Think how Job will feel afterwards! The words hurt Job because Eliphaz does not understand. If you want to be a better friend, learn from Eliphaz' mistakes!

1. DO NOT GIVE ANSWERS BEFORE YOU HAVE LISTENED

📖 *Job 4:2*

All Job has said is, "It hurts so much that I want to die!" **Job** probably has not yet understood what the real problem is. He is not ready to hear someone's advice! It is so easy for Eliphaz to see what he thinks the problem is, and to give out the answer. **But he is wrong, partly because he has not listened.**

> ⏩ *Listen, listen, listen. Then pray about what may help your friend.*

2. BE KIND

📖 *Job 4:1-6*

Job is in huge pain! Eliphaz is not kind to say this: "You have **given** so much good advice in the past. It is not so easy to **take** advice, is it!"

> ⏩ *Be kind! Even if you think they deserve what has happened, be kind!*

3. BE HUMBLE

📖 *Job 5:8*

Eliphaz thinks it is so easy! All you have to do is go back to God! Eliphaz needs to respect Job! Eliphaz should ask himself how **he** would feel, if all these things happened to **him**!

> ⏩ *Be humble! Even if you have the perfect Bible passage to say, be careful. It may seem easy and clear to you. But you are not the person in pain.*

4. DO NOT GET IT WRONG!

📖 *Job 4:7-8*

Even if Eliphaz were kind and humble, he still should not give advice, **because he has a wrong understanding of God!**

• Is Job 4:8 right? Is Job 4:7 right?

Eliphaz is **partly** right. God is fair. If we do evil, we will pay for it. But we will not always pay for it **in this life**. And he is wrong in Job 4:7. Many innocent people do suffer terrible things.

Eliphaz is wrong about Job, because he is wrong about God! Eliphaz thinks that Job's trouble is because Job has gone against God. He is wrong!

> ⏩ *Before you give advice, make sure that you understand the Bible well. Otherwise listen, be kind, pray—and ask someone else to help.*

7 WHY DO YOU ATTACK ME?

▣ Background

Job is hurt and surprised by his friend Eliphaz. Eliphaz wrongly thinks that Job must have done something bad. Eliphaz cannot see any other reason for Job's trouble.

Job thinks that he already has too much pain—and now his friends turn against him! Worse still, why has **God** turned against him?

📖 *Job 6 – 7* (**Notes** will help.)

⊙ Main point

Job **feels** that both God and his friends are against him. But God is certainly **not** against Job.

✦ Something to work on

Many Christians make the same mistake as Job. We **feel** that God is against us when instead he loves us just as much. God never told Job **why** he gave him so much trouble. This is because God wanted Job to **trust** him. God wants us to trust him too. He wants us to hold on to him when we do not understand and when we cannot feel him. This makes our faith strong in God. Job held on to God like this.

How can you best encourage your listeners to remember God's love and hold on to him?

Remember too that Jesus promises that we **will** have trouble in this world. The Bible gives us many important reasons for this trouble. We need to remember these reasons. (Examples: James 1:2-4, 2 Corinthians 1:3-4, Hebrews 12:7-11.)

▣ Notes

- **Job 6:2-7.** "Surely you (friends) can let me complain!"

- **Job 6:8-13.** "Please finish my life, God!"

- **Job 6:14-23.** "You (friends) disappoint me so much!"

- **Job 6:24-30.** "Friends, please be honest with me. Tell me clearly what I have done wrong!"

- **Job 7:1-11.** "Pity me (be sorry for me), God!"

- **Job 7:12-21.** "Why will you not leave me alone, God!"

FRIENDS, WHY ATTACK ME? 📖 *Job 6:14*

📖 ***Proverbs 17:17.*** Job is right! Friends should **always** be friends— even when we say wrong things. Friends need to come and help us, not attack us!

Eliphaz disappoints Job so much. Job hopes for his friends to bring comfort, but instead they bring him even more pain! It feels like a hot desert journey when you need water so much. At last, you come to a stream of water. But when you arrive, the stream is dry. That is so disappointing! (Job 6:15-21)

> ⏩ *Pray that you will be a real friend to people in trouble. It is not easy!*
>
> • *Ask for **God's love**. Then you will be kind. You will not disappoint your friend. Love will help them through their pain.*

GOD, WHY ATTACK ME? 📖 *Job 6:4*

Job feels that God is against him. It is as if God shoots angry arrows at him. Their poison spreads through his body. He cannot understand why his best Friend has turned against him! Is Job right?

We know that God **is** behind all the "arrows" of trouble. But we also know that God **is not** angry with Job! **Job misunderstands God's arrows.**

> ⏩ *This is very important for us. We often do not understand why bad things happen to us. **But they usually do not mean that God is against us.** We may feel God is far from us, but he has promised to be **with his people** in trouble. Hold on to God's promises to his people;* 📖 ***Isaiah 43:1-2.***

Job wrongly thinks that God is against him, but Job does not turn against God! He goes **to** God in his pain:

• Job asks God to finish his life, so that he will not go against his God; 📖 ***Job 6:8-10.***

• Job tells God how terrible he feels. He has no rest from pain; 📖 ***Job 7:4-5.***

• Job asks God to leave him alone. He asks, "Why does God watch me so much? Why does he give me all this attention?" 📖 ***Job 7:17-20***

> ⏩ *There is a good reason why God will not leave Job alone. It is the same for all God's people. **He loves us so much!** He plans all our "trouble" for our good. And he watches over us until we come through our pain to trust him and thank him.* 📖 ***Jeremiah 29:11***

8 SOMEONE TO SPEAK FOR ME!

▣ Background

Bildad replies to Job in Job 8, but he makes the same mistakes as Eliphaz. He says that if Job does what is good, he will know God's blessing. But Job **has** done what is good, and all this trouble came!

Job feels that no one will listen to him. He knows that God is always right, but God seems so far away. He needs someone to speak to God for him!

📖 *Job 9*

⊙ Main point

Job feels that God is too great for him. He wants someone to speak to God for him.

⊛ Something to work on

Remember that Job is in great pain. What he says is a mixture. Some things he says are right, some are not right. When we are in trouble, we are often like that!

This means that we have to take care as we read. We can learn from Job's feelings, even when Job is wrong.

▣ Notes

• **Job 9:14-20.** Job feels that he is "innocent" (not guilty). But God is so great that Job cannot argue with him! Job can only ask God for pity ("mercy"). Job does not believe that God will listen to him. He thinks that God will attack him again (Job 14:17-18). God is too strong for Job!

• **Job 9:30-31.** Job imagines a bath to wash away every spot of guilt. But he would still be guilty before a holy God. He would be as dirty as someone who came out of a dirty pit.

• **Job 9:32-35.** God is not a human, so Job cannot argue with him in court. He wants someone to come between him and God ("arbitrate"). He wants someone to speak to God, to take away God's anger.

GOD IS TOO GREAT FOR JOB

📖 *Job 9:14-20*

⊕ Imagine how you would feel if you complained to the leader of your country. You have important points to make, but he has so much power. It feels as if he will never listen. Job feels like that.

God is so great; 📖 *Job 9:4-10.* Job praises God because he is so great! God feels too strong for Job, but Job still praises his great God!

God is so holy; 📖 *Job 9:20, 30-31.* Job knows that he has done nothing bad to deserve his trouble. But Job also knows that he is a sinner before God. As soon as he opens his mouth, sin will come out!

So far, Job is right. But he makes a big mistake. He still thinks that God is against him. He thinks that God is so big that he will not listen to him. He thinks that God will not be fair. (This is wrong!)
📖 *Job 9:14-18*

> ⏩ *If we trust God, he is never "**too big for us**"! His power is not against us—it is for us! And God does not want us to feel guilty when we have done nothing wrong. God is always just and fair and kind. Job felt afraid of God—but when we trust God, we are **safe** in him.*

SOMEONE TO SPEAK FOR ME!

📖 *Job 9:32-35*

Job feels as if he is in court. He has done nothing wrong, but the judge says "guilty". He feels that he cannot argue against God. He wants someone else to speak for him. He wants someone to ask God to be kind to him and to listen to him.

Again, Job is **wrong about God**. Perhaps we make the same mistake. God is love! Job **can** talk to God and God is glad to listen! Job does not need someone else to make God kind! God will not listen more to someone else.

Job feels wrongly about God, but his words do speak truth that **points us to Jesus!** We are guilty before God, our Judge. So we **do** need someone to come between us and God. We need Jesus to ask God to forgive us. More than that, we need Jesus to **take** our guilt for us. This is why he died on the cross! 📖 *1 John 2:1-2*

> ⏩ *Praise God that, if we trust him, Jesus speaks for us! We have sinned, but Jesus says, "Do not fear, I took your guilt away. You have peace with God."*
>
> *Remember this when you cannot **feel** God's love. Remember that Jesus speaks for you, and so the Father smiles on you.*

9 DARK HOPE

◉ Background

The arguments with Job's friends continue. When Job talks, he says a lot about pain and death. He cannot understand why God has given him all this trouble. He feels very dark inside.

But sometimes there is a quick flash of light. Job thinks of something that gives him a little hope. Then the darkness returns. He feels miserable again.

See Job's hope in 📖 *Job 13:15* ("Though he slay me, yet will I hope in him") and *16:19*. Read the sections before and after these verses to see that Job still feels dark.

◉ Main point

Even in the darkest times, faith in God brings hope for the future.

◉ Something to work on

This message will help God's people who have **very little hope**, like Job. Do not preach as if Job has come out of his pain! Job does not have a clear faith here. He is desperate and in despair. But he somehow holds on to God. This is what gives him flashes of hope. He must believe that God will help him in the end.

Jeremiah feels like Job when God judges Jerusalem; 📖 *Lamentations 3:13-33.*

◉ Notes

• **Job 13:15.** "Even if he kills ("slays") me, I will hope in him." Job wants to speak out and say that he is innocent (Job 13:13). Even if God judges him with death, Job will put his trust in God.

• **Job 16:19.** Job still feels that God is against him (Job 16:14). God will not listen to him **on earth**. But one day, God will stand up for Job in **heaven**. God will be Job's "advocate" or "witness" to speak for him! At last things will be fair! (Again, Job speaks more truth than he knows. **Jesus** became the one to speak for his people in heaven [as in Job 9:33]).

HOPE, WHATEVER HAPPENS
📖 *Job 13:15*

⊕ Imagine that you are lost in the forest (bush). Then you see someone, but it is an old enemy. He throws stones at you, but you still follow him! It is the only way to get out of the forest!

It is like that for Job. He has no one to help him, except God. Job (wrongly) feels that God is against him, but God is still his only hope. Job speaks out. He feels that he must say that he is innocent. And he will trust God to hear him. Job does not feel that God is fair to him. He feels that God attacks him. But Job's only hope is to trust God to be fair! Job trusts God not to let him down in the end.

➧ *Put your hope in God, whatever happens! Even if the most terrible things happen to you, hold on to God! Expect God to help you, even when it feels as if he is against you. God never takes his love away from his people. God **will not** let you down when you trust him. Do not trust your feelings—trust in God and his promises.*

HOPE IN HEAVEN
📖 *Job 16:19*

Remember how dark and miserable Job feels! He has lost sight of God's love: 📖 *Job 16:9-14.*

• What does Job think of God now?

We can see how wrong Job is. We may feel upset if a believer says things like this. But sometimes God's people feel dark and depressed like this. Sometimes people get ill, so that they can only see bad things.

But in Job's pain there comes a flash of light. As Job thinks about God, he knows that God must be fair in the end! It feels as if God will not listen to him **now**. So Job believes that God will listen to him after he dies, when he meets God! Job imagines a court in heaven. In the court there is someone who will speak up for Job. And that person is God! Job is right—**Jesus** speaks up for his people.

➧ *So many things are unfair **now**. But one day, everything will be fair. And, if we know God, someone will speak up for us in heaven. **Jesus** will say, "I have died for their sins—they have peace with God!" God never promises that **now** everything will be right. But in heaven, Jesus will speak up for the people he loves. He will put everything right!*

10 MY REDEEMER!

◉ Background

This is another example of Job's "dark hope". Everyone is against him. He feels so hopeless and dark. Then, in his darkness, Job has a flash of hope. This saves him from complete despair. But his miserable feelings soon return. Darkness follows the flash of light.

📖 *Job 19:20-27*

◉ Main point

Job hopes in God, his "Redeemer" (Saviour). After death, Job will see God.

✦ Something to work on

Be careful with this section. Some of it is hard to translate from the Hebrew language. Also, in the Old Testament, people sometimes say more than they understand. It is easy for **us now** to see how Job points to Jesus and to the resurrection. We do not know how clearly Job saw these things. We do know that—

• Job hopes in God, his Redeemer, to save him.

• After death, Job knows that he will see God.

◉ Notes

• **Job 19:23-24.** Job's friends are unfair. They say that Job has sinned. They will not believe Job. So Job wants his words written down. He wants them "engraved" (deeply scratched) in rock, so that no one can rub them out. This is so that people will know the truth. Job wants people to know that he is innocent. (God gave Job what he wanted! His words are in the Bible.)

• **Job 19:25.** "I know that my Redeemer lives." A "redeemer" is someone who pays a price to make people free. Job hopes in his God to "redeem" (rescue) him. God will speak for him in heaven. God will end Job's trouble.

• **Job 19:26-27.** Job expects to see God after he has died. After death, Job expects to be a real man, with a real body and real eyes. (We know that Job will rise from the dead. He will have a perfect new body, ready for heaven.)

MY REDEEMER!

📖 *Job 19:25*

1. Hope comes when we remember who our God is.

Job has no hope when he looks at **his trouble**. Job's **friends** give him no hope. But Job has hope when he remembers **who God is**. God does not change. God **is** fair and loving and answers our cries for help. Job cannot **feel** God's love and care now, but he still trusts in "my Redeemer" to help him. He is sure that his God **will** redeem (rescue) him in the end.

> ⏩ *When you feel dark and have no hope, **remember who your God is**. His love lasts for ever (Jeremiah 31:3). God **will** help his people when they trust him. God is the Saviour-God, so he must save! Even when you die, your Redeemer-God lives—so you are safe in him.*

2. Hope comes when we remember who our Jesus is.

Job's words point us to **Jesus** the Saviour. Job may not see this, but we can see our Redeemer on the cross. We can see how much he loves his people, because he died for them.

> ⏩ *If Jesus died to save you, will he leave you now? That is impossible! You may feel dark, but do not look at yourself. Look up to Jesus! Hope in your Redeemer! He lives in heaven for you (Hebrews 7:25).*

MY LIFE AFTER DEATH!

📖 *Job 19:26-27*

If Job's Redeemer lives, then Job must live too! Job thinks that soon he will die, but death cannot be the end. If God is his Redeemer, then God will not let Job be apart from God for ever! So Job is sure that he will live, **after** his death. He is in great trouble now, but one day he will see God. What a wonderful thought that is!

The New Testament tells us clearly what Job saw from a distance. Jesus, the Redeemer, will return. God will raise everyone from the dead. Jesus will take believers with him. They will see Jesus as he is. They will be like him. They will have new bodies to enjoy God for ever!

📖 *1 John 3:2*

> ⏩ *If you do not know Jesus as your Redeemer, you have no hope. You may be in trouble now, but there is much worse trouble to come. Go to Jesus now!*

> ⏩ *If you do know Jesus as your Redeemer, you have great hope! Your big trouble now is really a small thing. Soon Jesus will come for you. All your pain will be over. Do not give up—hope in your resurrection!*
> 📖 *I Thessalonians 4:16-18*

11 GOD HAS GOOD REASONS!

◉ Background

Job's friends continue to accuse Job of some great sin. They tell him to turn back to God. They say that then God will bless Job; 📖 *Job 22:21-26.*

But God seems to have left Job when he has not sinned. Job cries out to God, but God does not answer. Job's biggest pain is that he cannot find God: 📖 *Job 23:1-12.*

In his pain, Job knows that God has a reason for it; 📖 *Job 23:10.*

◉ Main point

God may feel far away, but trust him! He has good reasons for our suffering.

✱ Something to work on

Often Christians do the **wrong things** in their suffering. They may stop praying. They may turn away from God. They may be in despair and even try to kill themselves. They may drink a lot of alcohol.

Job helps us to do the **right thing** when God will not answer. Help your listeners to learn from Job. Even in deep trouble, he never gave up. Instead, he trusted that God has reasons for his pain. Good things will come out of it.

◉ Notes

- **Job 23:4-7.** This shows one reason why Job wants to find God. Job will tell God that he does not deserve this suffering! Earlier, Job did not think that God would listen (Job 9:14-20). Now he feels that God would be fair to him.

- **Job 23:10.** "When he has tested me, I shall come forth (out) as gold." (This is the right translation.) Job remembers that gold goes through fire for good reasons. Job looks past his trouble and sees that good things will come from it.

- **Job 23:11-12.** Job can say this about his life! He feels that God will see that this is true. God will see that he is innocent (he does not deserve these bad things).

WHERE IS GOD?

📖 *Job 23:3*

Some people turn **away** from God when trouble comes. They try to get on with life without God. Job is not like that. He knows that he **must have God**. Job cannot live without God.

But Job cannot find God. He cries to God, but God is silent.

⊕ When you lose something important, you look everywhere. You do nothing else until you find it. Job is like that; 📖 *Job 23:8-9*. (God will come to Job in the end! Job 38:1.)

> ⏩ *Are you like Job? You cannot live without God? Do not give up. Look for him until you find him. Remember what Jesus promises;* 📖 *Matthew 7:7-8.*

GOD HAS GOOD REASONS

📖 *Job 23:10*

- Remember that when you cannot find God, **he has not lost you!**

- Remember that when you understand nothing, **God knows everything!**

It can be hard when we do not see **why** bad things happen to us. It does not make sense to us! But if God knows, we do not **need** to know. God has a good reason for our trouble. We only need to put our hand in God's hand. He will lead us through the darkness.

We may not know why God has done this particular thing, but God does **tell us some good reasons** for trouble. We must be like Job and remember God's reasons; 📖 *Job 23:10* (see translation in **Notes**).

- **God tests his "gold"** (his precious people) **to show that it is real gold.** Some people look like Christians until trouble comes. But we know that Job was not like that. He was real gold. Fire cannot damage real gold. Trouble cannot hurt true Christians in the end. **It only proves that they are real and true;** 📖 *1 Peter 1:6-7*.

- **God tests his "gold" to make it pure.** Fire makes gold better! God uses trouble to make his people pure; 📖 *Romans 5:3-4*.

> ⏩ *God may feel so far away, but remember that **he has good reasons** for your trouble. He wants people to see how **real your faith is**. And he wants to **make you pure**. Do you want these things?*
>
> ⏩ *Pray for God's help to accept his loving gift of pain. Do not fight against it, but trust God to bring you through it.* 📖 *James 1:12*

12 WHERE IS WISDOM?

⊡ Background

Job and his three friends have argued for a long time. At last the three friends have finished. But they have not helped Job. There were many words, but little wisdom.

Job 28 is different! It is not a difficult argument. Job does not talk about his pain. Instead, Job gives us some wise words about wisdom.

📖 *Job 28*

⊡ Main point

You find wisdom when you fear (honour) the Lord.

⊛ Something to work on

Wisdom is not about **what we know**. It is about **who we know** and **how we live**. Job 28:28 is very important, especially in a time of trouble. We do not need to answer all our questions. We do not need to know **why** God has brought us hard times. We **do** need to continue to honour God and live for him. Try to learn and remember Job 28:28.

We see God's wisdom best in Jesus' death for sinners. This looks foolish to most people, but the cross is where we can know God. The cross is where we begin a wise life.

📖 *1 Corinthians 1:22-24, Colossians 2:3.*

⊛ Notes

- **Job 28:1-11.** Man can find silver, gold and precious stones. Man searches the deepest parts of the earth to find valuable treasure.

- **Job 28:12-19.** But man cannot find wisdom! He cannot find it in the earth or the sea. He cannot buy wisdom with gold. Wisdom is more valuable than everything.

- **Job 28:20-28.** Where does wisdom come from? No one knows— except God (Job 28:23). And God has told man where to find wisdom! (Job 28:28) You find wisdom when you "fear" (honour, show big respect for, worship) God. You find wisdom when you turn from ("shun") wrong things.

MAN CANNOT FIND WISDOM

Man is very good at finding things. Thousands of years ago, when Job was alive, man could find gold and precious stones in deep mines (pits);
📖 *Job 28:10-11. [Give examples of how scientific instruments like microscopes help us today to see many hidden things.]*

But man cannot find wisdom;
📖 *Job 28:12-15.*

• Why is wisdom more valuable than gold?

• Why is it impossible for man to find wisdom?

Man wants to find the answers to all the difficult questions, but God hides the answers. God does not want us to know everything. Many things are only for God to know;
📖 *Deuteronomy 29:29.*

Job and his friends argue for a long time. But they still do not understand why Job suffers so much. They look for answers. But they have not found wisdom. Job 28 will show how to get wisdom.

GOD SHOWS US WISDOM
📖 *Job 28:20, 23, 28*

⊕ You look for something for hours. You cannot find it anywhere. Then you realise that it was in your pocket all the time!

Wisdom is not hard to find if we look in the right place! We do not need to ask lots of difficult questions. We only need to ask **God** for wisdom (James 1:5).

And Job already had this wisdom!
📖 *Job 1:1, 28:28*

• How can Job be wise in his pain?

Job does not need to ask **why** God has done this to him. Job only needs to trust God and live for God, as before. This is wisdom!

Wisdom is not about knowing why. Wisdom is about knowing God.

> ⯈ *When Job looks at his God, not at his pain, he sees the wise way to live. When you have trouble, remember Job 28:28! Job only needed to trust and honour God as he did before the trouble came. So do we! Continue to **fear** God and **say no** to wrong thoughts and actions. This is wisdom!*

Wisdom is the most valuable thing in the world. Praise God if he has shown you the wise way to live! Many people look in the wrong place, but God has shown us where to find true wisdom. That place is the cross of Jesus;
📖 *1 Corinthians 1:22-24.*
Do you know true wisdom?

13 GODLY LIFE!

▣ Background

Job 31 has Job's last words to his friends. Many times Job has said, "I am innocent". He has done nothing to deserve punishment. Here Job shows us his godly life. Before God, Job says that he has not sinned in this way or that way. His life fits what he said in 📖 *Job 28:28.* It also fits what God said in 📖 *Job 1:8.*

▣ Main point

Job is a great example of a godly life.

⊠ Something to work on

Sin with sex spoils many lives and families. Think how you can encourage people to follow Job's example. How can we keep our eyes and minds pure? How can we keep our actions right?

It is easy to agree with Job's example, but what tempts people to sin with sex? How can you encourage your listeners to say no to wrong thoughts at the beginning? Do they need to make a promise to God, like Job? Do they need to ask a friend to help them?

▣ Notes

Many times in Job 31, Job writes like this: "If I have done this wrong thing, let that terrible thing happen to me." Job means: "I have **never done** this wrong thing". If this is not true, he wants God to make it clear.

- **Job 31:1.** "lustfully"—in a wrong, sexual way. Job knew that sexual sin begins with a look. So he made a "covenant" (strong promise) not to look in a wrong way.

- **Job 31:5.** "falsehood", "deceit"— lies, not honest.

- **Job 31:7.** "If my heart has been led by my eyes". First you **look**, then you **want** something that is wrong, then you **get** it. Job has not done this!

- **Job 31:9.** "If my heart has been "enticed" (attracted) by a woman, or if I have "lurked" (waited, hidden) at her door…"

- **Job 31:16-23.** Job has always cared for poor people (16), shared food with hungry people (17-18). He has given clothes to people in need (19-20), been fair to people who have no one to help them (21). If he has not done this, then let his arm fall off! (22). He has not done wrong because he was afraid of God's punishment (23).

PURE  *Job 31:1, 9-10*

• Where does sin with sex begin?

Girls can be too friendly with men. Men can think of pretty women and let their thoughts go on. This is wrong, but sin starts before these things. Job knew that sexual sin starts with a **look**.

• It is not wrong to look at someone! What **is** wrong? What did Job make a promise never to do?

> ➡ *Matthew 5:28-29. Ask God to forgive you for wrong thoughts and actions. Ask God to help you not to **look** in a wrong way. What do you need to do so that you do not sin with sex?*

HONEST

HE NEVER CHEATS
Job 31:5-8

Many people will try to cheat a little if no one sees. But Job knows who **always** sees (Job 31:4). Job never cheats. He wants God to weigh him to show that he is honest! If Job is wrong (if he is a cheat), then let people steal all his crops!

HE IS FAIR TO HIS SERVANTS
Job 31:13-15

• Not many people were fair to servants! So why does **Job** listen when they complain?

> ➡ *It is easy to be like everyone else. But God calls his people to be different. What have you learned from Job's example?*

CARING *Job 31:16-23*

We all know that it is wrong to do bad things. Do you know that it is also wrong **not to do good things** (James 4:17)?

Job knew this. He was rich and could help people in need. He knew that God watched him. Did Job tell people to go away? Did Job look the other way when he saw someone who needed help?

> ➡ *Are you a friend to people who need help? You may not be rich like Job, but think what God wants you to do to care for other people?*

Job is a great example—and he reminds us of an even greater example. Jesus **always** did **everything** to please his Father in heaven. We feel sad that our lives are not like Jesus' life, or even Job's. But do not give up! Jesus came to live a perfect life for sinners like us! Jesus' perfect life becomes ours when we trust him! God looks at us and sees Jesus' perfect life! So God **accepts** us in Jesus! Praise him!

14 LESSONS FROM GOD'S GREATNESS

⬡ Background

Job's three friends have no more to say. Job has no more to say. But someone else has listened to everything. **Elihu** has a lot to say! (Job 32 – 37)

At first, Elihu is sure that **he** has all the answers! He is angry with Job and his friends. He wants them to listen to his wisdom. 📖 *Job 32: 1-3, 33:1-3.* But Elihu's wisdom is no better. Like the three friends, Elihu does not understand Job. Like them, Elihu thinks that Job must deserve his trouble (Job 34:5-12).

But then, Elihu stops thinking about his own wisdom. Instead, he thinks about how great God is. So Elihu has important lessons to teach; 📖 *Job 36:22 – 37:24.*

⬡ Main point

We become wise when we think about God's greatness and become humble.

⬡ Something to work on

Many people are afraid of storms. Christians should remember that God is in control. He sends storms. So there is no need to be afraid. Instead, we should praise God for his greatness and power. We should feel small, but not afraid.

⊕ A Christian sailor enjoyed the big storm at sea. His wife was really frightened. Her husband smiled and looked at their baby sleeping peacefully in her arms. "Look at how safe and secure our son feels in your arms. He is not worried by the storm. Should you not feel safe in the arms of God? Can you not trust your heavenly father who holds the storm in his hands?"

⬡ Notes

• **Job 36:24.** "extol"—praise.

• **Job 36:27 – 37: 3-4, 13, 15.** This long section describes God's control over a storm. It is **God** who sends lightning and thunder. It is under His control.

• **Job 37:21.** The sun comes out after the storm. It is too bright to look at.

LESSONS FROM GOD'S GREATNESS

Wisdom is not about knowing **why**. It is about knowing **God**. When we think about God's greatness we do not always get answers to our questions. But our problems do find their right place.

⊕ The leader of a country always looked up at the stars before he went to bed. That did not answer his problems! But it did remind him that God's greatness in creation was much bigger than his problems.

A **storm** helped Elihu to see God's greatness; 📖 *Job 37:10-14.*

1. REMEMBER TO PRAISE GOD
📖 *Job 36:24-26*

⊕ A Christian woman was so sad after her husband died. So she stopped singing. She soon saw that was wrong! God **always** deserves our praise!

Job praised God right at the beginning (Job 1:20-21). But sometimes, after weeks of trouble, we can forget to praise God. Stop to think how great God is—and praise him!

2. WE DO NOT KNOW MUCH
📖 *Job 37:5, 14-15*

Next time there is a storm, stop to think how little you know of God's ways. He controls the weather all over the world. But we do not know what he is doing. In our lives, God sends many different things. But we do not know God's plans.

3. GOD HAS MANY DIFFERENT PLANS
📖 *Job 37:13*

Look at the two different reasons for rain! God can use the same thing to show love or anger. He can use trouble to correct us or to bless us. Or both at the same time! Job's friends were sure that God sent trouble to punish Job. But God's plans were to bless Job! Remember that God's plans for his people are **always** to do them good.

4. AFTER THE STORM COMES THE SUN
📖 *Job 37:21*

The sun is just as strong as the storm—but very different. After trouble comes blessing for God's people. And God's smile is as strong as his storm.

> ⊳ *We need to look **away** from our troubles. Instead, we need to think about how great God is. Then we will be humble and more ready to trust God. We know so little, but God is in complete control. As with the weather, God sends what we need.* 📖 *1 Peter 5:6-7*

15 GOD SPEAKS

▣ Background

Neither Job nor God answers Elihu. But, as Elihu speaks about God's greatness, he prepares the way for **God** himself to speak. Out of a storm, God tests Job with many difficult questions.

📖 *Job 38 – 39.* God asks Job questions that make Job feel how small he is before God (Where were you..? Have you ever given orders...? What is the way to...? Can you...? Do you know...?)

📖 *Job 40:1-5.* Job is ashamed to answer God.

God wants to make Job even more humble. There are two more chapters of questions (Job 40 – 41). At last, in Job 42, Job says sorry to God.

▣ Main point

God makes Job feel how little he knows about God's ways.

✳ Something to work on

Sometimes, like Job, we feel that we need God's comfort. But when God speaks to Job, he speaks in a **storm** (Job 38:1). He does not comfort Job. He shows Job where he has gone wrong.

- What mistakes do Christians often make when they suffer? (We can feel sorry for ourselves, or think that God is unfair, or...)

- How does Job 38 – 39 help us with these mistakes?

▣ Notes

- **Job 38:2.** This means: "Who is this that questions my wisdom with 'ignorant' words that understand nothing?"

- **Job 38:3.** "Brace yourself"—stand up to me.

- **Job 40:2.** "Contends"—argues. Job has argued with God. Job has accused God. He has suggested that God was not fair to him. So now let Job answer God!

WHO ARE YOU?
📖 *Job 38:1-3*

⊕ I will always remember three words that a man spoke to me at college. "Who are you?" He was not friendly. The meaning was very clear. He wanted me to get out! Those three words made me feel so small!

God asks Job, "Who are you"? God wants Job to see how small he is. God wants Job to see how little he understands. But God is **not** being unkind! In fact, God wants Job to come back into friendship with him. What God says is not comfortable for Job—but remember how much Job wanted God to speak to him! It shows that God has not left Job!

Job has asked many questions about God. He has not trusted God's wisdom and fairness. But who is Job to doubt God? Job has no right to think that God could be wrong! It is time for God to ask the questions—but will Job be able to answer them?

⟫ *Do you think that God should answer your questions? Perhaps you suffer a lot—but that does not give you the right to know what God is doing. Who are you? We must remember how great God is and how small we are.*

WHERE WERE YOU?
📖 *Job 38:4-18*

⊕ Imagine that you have a two-year-old child. What if she has to answer university exam questions! Impossible! She will never know the answers!

God asks Job question after question that Job cannot answer. *[Talk more about some of the questions.]* The only person who can do all these things is God! That is God's point. God wants Job to see how little he **knows**. God wants Job to see how little **power** he has;
📖 *Job 38:34-35.*

⟫ *There is such a big gap between God and us! We know so little! But sometimes, like Job, we say too much. We talk as if we know better than God does! We may think that if we were God, we would never do things the same way. God shows us here how foolish we are.*

SILENCE! 📖 *Job 40:1-5*

It is Job's turn to speak. Let him argue with God! Here is Job's chance at last. Let him tell God why it is unfair to make him suffer!

But Job has nothing to say. He knows that he has already said far too much. He knows how foolish his words have been. He will keep quiet and listen to God some more. Perhaps we can learn from Job...

16 GOD SPEAKS AGAIN

⊡ Background

God has more to say to Job. Job is humble and silent, but God wants more than this. God wants Job to see how wrong some of his thoughts about God were. God wants Job to say sorry and come back to him.

- Job should never think that God is unfair; 📖 *Job 40:6-14.*

- God is much more powerful than the great behemoth and leviathan. First let Job make these frightening animals his pets! **Then**, if he dares, Job can stand up to God! 📖 *Job 40:15 – 41:34*

⊙ Main point

God is much greater than we think. We should never argue with him. We should never think that God is unfair.

⊛ Something to work on

We can be so proud. We can so quickly think that we know better than God. Pray about how to use these chapters to show your listeners how foolish this is. How small we are! How great God is! Our doubts and questions about God's ways come from our poor understanding of God.

⊡ Notes

- **Job 40:8.** These are God's main questions for Job. They mean: "Will you try to prove that I am unjust? Will you try to make me wrong so that you can be right?"

- **Job 40:9-14.** Does Job think he is as strong and magnificent as God? Then let him show it! Let Job act as God! Let Job judge proud and wicked men and bring them down!

- **Job 40:15, 41:1.** "Behemoth" and "leviathan". The Behemoth sounds a bit like a hippopotamus. The leviathan is a bit like a big crocodile. But both animals sound bigger and fiercer than a hippopotamus and a crocodile. They may have been dinosaurs (animals that no longer exist).

- **Job 41:10.** The leviathan is much too fierce to have as a pet! No one is strong enough to control him! So no one is strong enough to stand against **God**, who made the leviathan!

GOD IS RIGHT!

📖 *Job 40:6-14*

⊕ Some people say, "When I meet God, I will have some questions to ask him!" Are they right?

Job had really wanted to find God. He wanted to ask God some questions. He wanted to ask if God was fair to give him all this pain. **But when God meets Job, it is God who asks all the questions!**

Job could not understand why God gave him all this suffering. Job knew that he had done nothing to deserve it. Then Job made his mistake. If **he** had done nothing wrong, he could not see how **God** was fair to do all this!

Job has asked questions about God. It is time for Job to answer God's question! 📖 *Job 40:8*

> ⨠ *Do you ever think or say, "God, you are not fair"? That is the wrong way to think. God is always fair. It is impossible for God to be unjust (Deuteronomy 32:4). Our problem is that **we** do not understand. Like Job, we only see a little of what God is doing. We are not God!*

God gives Job a test. Let Job show that he can be God! Let Job bring down proud, evil men and give them what they deserve! Or, if Job cannot do this, let God decide what is fair! 📖 *Job 40:9-14*

GOD IS GOD!

📖 *Job 41:1-10*

God gives Job another test. If Job can do this, then he is strong enough to ask God his questions. Job must catch a leviathan and lead him with string! He must control him and make him tame, like a pet dog! This is impossible—unless you are God! The leviathan is so fierce that no one comes near him.

📖 *Job 41:10.* God has made his point. Job is not like God. He is weak and tiny and knows very little. If Job is afraid to argue with a leviathan, he should be much more afraid to argue against God.

So Job never gets answers to his questions. (Why me? Is it fair?) But God shows him that he does not **need** those answers. Instead, Job needs to trust that God is God, and God is fair and just.

> ⨠ *It can be very hard to understand how God is fair. Often things do not look fair to us. Remember the lessons from these chapters! Are you big and strong enough to argue against God? Can you do the things that God can do? If not, then **trust** God to be God. **Trust** God to be just. And wait for Jesus the Judge to return. He will make everything right!*

17 LESSONS LEARNED

◉ Background

Why does Job have to suffer for so long?

It is because God wants Job to learn some valuable lessons. The lessons come from all the suffering and also from God's words to Job (Job 38 – 41).

See how different Job is after his suffering; 📖 *Job 42:1-6.*

◉ Main point

Job is humble before God. He is sorry for too many foolish words.

⊛ Something to work on

When we suffer, we really want the trouble to stop! The book of Job shows us that often the suffering goes on and on. Only then do we learn the special things that God wants to show us. We must learn to be patient when we suffer. We need to wait for God to bring us out of trouble, in his time.

📖 *James 5:10-11*

◉ Notes

• **Job 42:2.** God has the right and the power to do anything he wants. No one can stop ("thwart") God's plans. Job knew this before, but now he is **glad** that it is true.

• **Job 42:3.** Job answers God's question (Job 38:2). He sees that he has said too much about God's ways. God's ways are too "wonderful" (big) for him to understand.

• **Job 42:5.** Job feels that now he really **knows** God in a much deeper way. Before, it was as if he only **heard** about God. But now God has come close to him.

• **Job 42:6.** Job "repents". He sees that he has said wrong things in his pain. He "despises" (hates) those things. He is ashamed of what he has said and says sorry.

LESSONS LEARNED

1. GOD DOES WHAT HE WANTS
📖 *Job 42:2*

We know that this is true, but sometimes we do not like it. Perhaps we wish that we could stop some things. But we know that no one can stop God's plans.

Job always knew that God does what he wants. But he has learned to **praise** God for this in a new way. He is glad that he cannot stop God's plans—even when they are so painful! Do you agree with Job?

2. WE KNOW SO LITTLE
📖 *Job 42:3*

We like to think that we are experts! We talk about God's ways as if we know so much! Then God, the real expert, speaks. He knows everything and we feel so small.

- Have you sometimes been like Job? Have you said too much about God's ways?

- What are some of the things that we do not understand about God?

3. WE NEED TO KNOW GOD
📖 *Job 42:5*

We can all talk **about** God. Job knew so much **about** God. But now he **knows** God in a new way. Job's suffering has made him "see" (know) God better.

- Has suffering brought you closer to God? *[You could ask some people to share what their suffering has taught them about God.]*

- Do you want to know Jesus better? Are you willing to suffer? 📖 *Philippians 3:10.*

4. WE NEED TO REPENT
📖 *Job 42:6*

Job is sorry and ashamed of what he has said about God. So he **turns back to God** ("repents"). He does not doubt God any more. He does not want to argue with him. He does not think that God is unfair. Instead, he **trusts** God's wisdom and love.

> ⟫ *We know that Job's suffering was not God's punishment for sin. Our suffering too is often not **because** we have done wrong. It is not a punishment.*
>
> *But, like Job, it is so easy to sin **in** our suffering. It is hard to accept the trouble. It is hard to trust that God still loves us. So, like Job, we think and say wrong things about God. Do you need to say sorry to God and turn back to him? What lessons does God want you to learn?*

18 GOD'S BLESSING!

⊡ Background

God has turned Job back to him. Job is glad to trust God. So it is time for God to bless Job! God does not want Job to suffer any longer than is necessary.

He gives Job even more than he had at first! This shows everyone clearly that God loves Job. It shows that Job has done right to hold on to God through his suffering.

📖 *Job 42:7-17*

⊡ Main point

God's people may suffer for a while, but God always plans good things for his people.

⊠ Something to work on

Job's story has the perfect ending. Everything goes right for him. But it is not often like this for God's people. Usually we have problems all through our lives. Most Christians are not rich like Job! But we must remember that our story **does** have the perfect ending if we belong to God. Job's story points us to the perfect ending of heaven. It teaches us that all the suffering will one day end. Then we will know **only** God's blessing.

⊡ Notes

• **Job 42:7.** Job said **some** wrong things about God. But it was still mostly "right". Job's friends were so sure about what was wrong with Job that they did not see what was wrong with **their** words. They spoke a lot of wrong against Job and God. Now Job must pray for them.

• **Job 42:7-9.** God was angry with Job's friends, but see that he wanted them too to come back to him. Job's suffering taught his friends important lessons. (Examples: God's ways are too big to understand, bad things do happen to good people...)

• **Job 42:10.** "Prosperous"—rich. God's blessing does not mean that we will be rich and healthy. Job's riches are a picture of the real blessings God has for his people. God gives his people love, peace, joy and forgiveness through Jesus. Then heaven! These are much better than money and possessions!

• **Job 42:11.** Job's suffering affected many people. They could all learn how God uses suffering to do his people good.

God is always good! It was hard to see this through Job's suffering. Here we can see God's goodness towards Job and his friends.

GOD 📖 *Job 42:10, 12*

Sometimes we ask, "Why do bad things happen to God's people?" God's answer is that he **only** has good plans for his people (Jeremiah 32:40).

Praise God that—

• God **uses** bad things for our good. Our trouble is not wasted. Those years when we were ill were not wasted. What good things does suffering bring?

• God loves to bless his people more and more. God gives twice as much to Job to show how much he loves him. If life seems hard now, remember God's plan of heaven! (2 Corinthians 4:17)

FRIENDS 📖 *Job 42:7-9, 11*

⊕ At the moment, I am ill with cancer. God has loving plans in this for me and my family. But he also has spoken to many **other people**. They too have thought a lot about their lives and their deaths. Praise God that he can use our suffering to bless many people.

Job's three friends were sure that they knew the problem with Job. But God made them see how **they** were wrong. He humbled them and forgave them. It was hard for them to ask Job to pray for them! But God used this to teach them many things about God.

• What lessons do you think Job's friends and relatives learned?

JOB 📖 *Job 42:7, 8, 12*

Job learns many things through his suffering. But notice how the book ends as it began.

• Job is a **good** man. He lives right and speaks right (Job 1:1, 42:7). Job was not perfect. But God trusted Job to hold on to him through his suffering.

• Job is a **blessed** man (Job 1:2-3, 42:12). It was hard to see blessing in his suffering. But, in the end, blessing comes when we trust God.

> ⊗ *Do you want to know God's blessing? Remember that God's good plans always come to his people! Like Job, never let go of God! Never think that it is better to do things your own way. Even if it hurts so much, remember Job. Remember that God plans great blessing for you.*

E: LESSONS FROM JOB

It is important to take lessons from God's word into our lives. It will help your people to discuss these questions in groups and pray about them. The questions help us to learn some of the main lessons from this book. You can use these questions after you have finished all your talks on Job. Or you may want to use them after each section.

Lessons from Job

1. God is in control, not Satan!

• What happened to Satan's evil plans for Job?

• Are you afraid of Satan or evil spirits? What have you learned from Job's story?

2. God is always good and always fair.

• How does Job learn this lesson?

• How can we hold on to this truth when things feel unfair?

3. God only has good plans for his people.

• Why is this true?

• When "bad" things happen, what things must we remember about God?

4. God works "bad" and painful things for the good of his people.

• How was this true for Job and his friends?

• Share how God has done this in your life.

5. There is so much we cannot understand, because we are not God.

• God never explained to Job why he had to suffer. Why is this?

• How does it help to remember who we are?

6. We do not need to understand everything. We do need to trust God in everything.

• In the end, why was Job happy not to understand?

• Think of examples in life. When do we need to trust more than to understand? (Example: young children and their parents.) How do the examples help us to trust God?

7. Knowing God is more important than knowing why.

• In what ways did Job (and Job's friends) know God better by the end?

• If your troubles mean that you know God better, are you happy to suffer?

8. God has many reasons for suffering. All of them are good.

• What are some of those reasons?

• Do you remember God's good reasons when trouble comes? How does that help?

9. The devil tries to use our suffering to turn us away from God. God uses our suffering to turn us to God.

• Think how both Satan and God gave Job his troubles. What were their different reasons?

• Some people turn away from God when they suffer. This is what the devil wants for us all. How can we help each other to turn to God in trouble?

10. Our suffering is often not because of our sin.
- What were the reasons for Job's suffering?
- What are some of the reasons God may bring suffering to your life?

11. It is very easy to sin when we suffer.
- Job held on to God, but what did he need to say sorry for?
- What sins do we need to watch out for when we suffer?

12. When we comfort people who are suffering, we need help from God.
- What mistakes did Job's friends make?

- What have you learned from their mistakes?
- What do you need to pray for, so that you can be a helpful friend?

13. Our suffering will not last for ever (if we trust in Jesus, who suffered for his people). God has the final answer to suffering. Suffering will end and heaven will come!
- When Job suffered, what did he think would happen to him? What did happen to him?
- When we have trouble, how does it help us to think about Jesus and about heaven?

Reasons for suffering

A talk or Bible study on this subject will help your listeners a lot. Think how best you can use the help below.

One of the hardest things about suffering is when we do not know **why** it has happened. Often God does not explain why. He wants us to trust him in our trouble.

But the Bible does give us many good reasons for trouble! God uses trouble in our lives to produce good things. When we suffer, we need to remember these reasons.

1. Suffering is part of the sinful world that we live in. Romans 8:22-23

From when Adam sinned, the whole world has been in trouble. Sin brought trouble to everyone. Everyone knows illness, pain, disappointment and death. In Romans 8,

Paul tells us that the whole of creation "groans" (hurts) because sin made everything go wrong.

Christians have to live in this spoiled world of sin! We have trouble, like everyone else. But we look forward to a day when all the trouble of this world will be gone. We look forward to heaven, where there will be no more pain.

2. Suffering may be our own fault

Perhaps we are sick because we drank some dirty water. This is not from God, but from us! Perhaps we made a bad decision that brought us trouble. This is our fault! We must learn lessons from our mistakes. We can ask God to help us through the trouble that we make for ourselves.

3. Suffering may be God's correction. Hebrews 12:4-13

Notice that Hebrews 12 says that God is a

loving Father to his children. He is not cruel and angry. He does not like to hurt us (Lamentations 3:31-33). If we trust in Jesus, suffering is not God's punishment. Jesus has suffered on the cross for all our sin! Like a good father, God wants us to go in the right way.

If we go away from God, he may use suffering to bring us back. Sometimes we will not listen to His word. Sometimes we will only listen when life hurts us. God sends us trouble because he loves us and wants us to turn to him again. If we ask him, God will show us when this is the reason for our trouble. Do not feel guilty when you have not gone away from God!

Like a Father, God uses suffering to train us. He gives us hard things so that we will learn lessons. He wants his children to grow up!

4. Suffering makes us grow in our faith. James 1:2-4, 12, Job 23:10

This is very often why God gives his people trouble. We often do not grow very well when life is easy. Trouble is like good soil to help plants grow. Trouble teaches us to trust God. Trouble makes us "mature" (grown up) and complete, not lacking anything. Job saw that trouble will make his faith like gold. James tells us to be glad when trouble comes because trouble makes our faith grow! We must not complain. We must trust that trouble is God's good gift to us.

5. Suffering can bring us closer to our suffering Saviour. Philippians 3:10

Paul wanted to share more in his Saviour's suffering. Paul knew that as he suffers he will know Jesus better.

6. Suffering can be persecution. Matthew 5:10-12

We suffer persecution because we are like Jesus and tell other people about Jesus. Jesus tells us to be glad when people hurt us because of him. It encourages us that we have become like Jesus. People hate us because they hate Jesus. We belong to Jesus.

7. Suffering can teach other people many things.

Today I read a card written to someone who is seriously ill. The card said that "your faith and patience in trouble has encouraged me a lot". The way we suffer can help other people. It can help them to keep going in their own trouble. It can make them think about the way they live.

One big reason for Job's suffering was to help millions of believers who read his book!

8. Suffering can help us to comfort other people. 2 Corinthians 1:3-7

Job's friends could not help to comfort Job—they did not understand suffering. But when God has comforted us in our suffering, we can help other people. We will be gentle and kind. They know that we understand their pain. We can tell them how good God has been to us.

Think how good all these reasons are! We find it hard to suffer now. But when we remember the good things that suffering brings, we can praise and trust God.